CRIME SCENE INVESTIGATION

FOOTPRINTS AND TIRE TRACKS

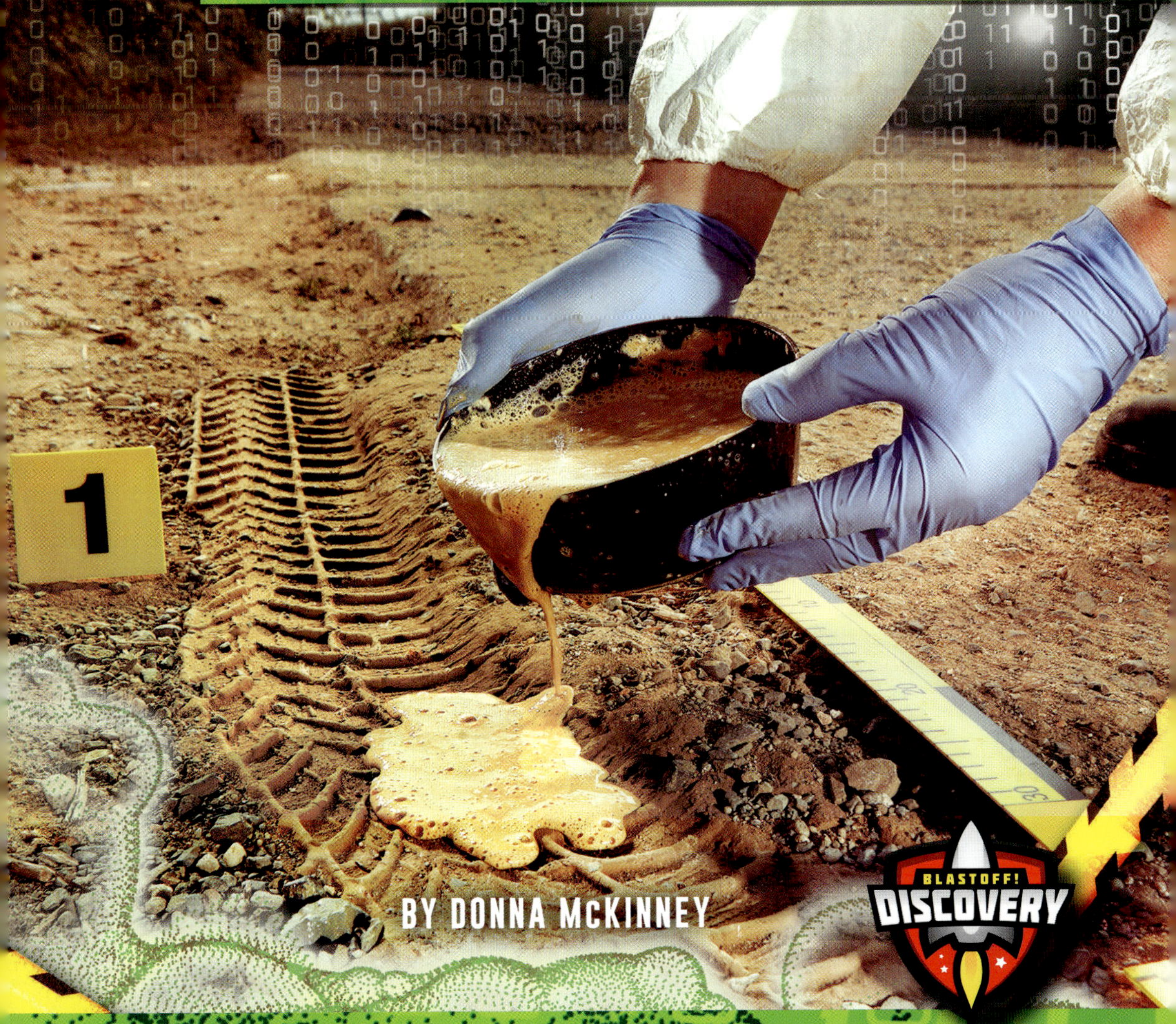

BY DONNA McKINNEY

BLASTOFF! DISCOVERY

LASTOFF! DISCOVERY, AN IMPRINT OF BELLWETHER MEDIA BY FLUTTERBEE

This edition first published in 2027 by Bellwether Media, Inc.

For information regarding permission, write to Bellwether Media, Inc., Attention: Permissions Department,
3500 American Blvd W, Suite 150, Bloomington, MN 55431.

Library of Congress Cataloging-in-Publication Data is available at www.loc.gov or upon request from the publisher.

ISBN: 9798898800819 (hardcover)
ISBN: 9798898802059 (ebook)

Editor: Rachael Barnes Series Designer: Josh Brink

Printed in the United States of America, North Mankato, MN.

TABLE OF CONTENTS

WHAT IS FOOTPRINT AND TIRE TRACK FORENSICS?

Early humans learned to follow tracks left by animals. These tracking skills helped them hunt prey and travel safely. Modern humans use tracking skills to solve crimes.

In 1786, a court case accepted shoe print **evidence** for the first time. Police made a paper cutout of a shoe print from the crime scene. Comparing different shoes to the cutout pointed to a **suspect**. The Federal Bureau of Investigation (FBI) first used footprint and tire track evidence in the early 1930s.

Today, **crime scene investigators** (CSIs) look for several details at crime scenes, including footprints and tire tracks. These unique marks are known as pattern evidence.

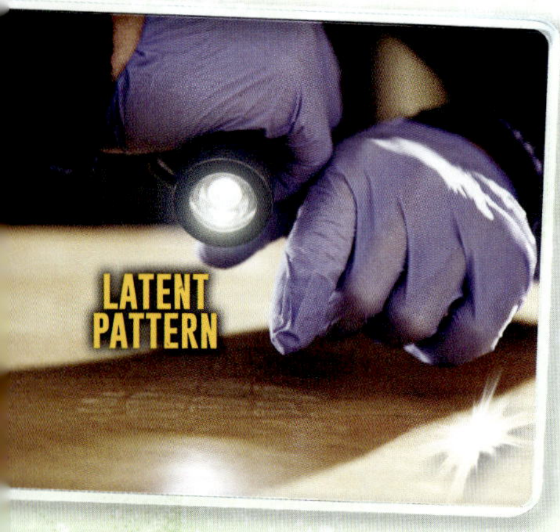

Footprints and tire tracks are the most common types of pattern evidence. They can be left at the scene in three different ways. Visible patterns are **2D** prints. Muddy footprints or muddy tire tracks left on hard surfaces are visible patterns. Plastic patterns are **3D** prints left in soft surfaces. These are found in carpet, sand, snow, or mud.

Latent patterns cannot be seen easily. These patterns are often left on smooth surfaces. CSIs use special tools to see latent prints. Patterns link suspects to a crime scene.

STATS

ANCIENT FOOTPRINTS

OLDEST HUMAN FOOTPRINTS

3.6 million years old

FREQUENCY OF FOOTPRINTS

Found at about **40 percent** of crime scenes

NUMBER OF PUBLIC FORENSIC CRIME LABS IN THE UNITED STATES

400

AT THE CRIME SCENE

CSIs collect crime scene evidence. Footprints are commonly found in investigations. Both footprint and tire track patterns tell a story about what happened at the scene. CSIs look for how many people were there. They try to see which direction suspects traveled.

Footprints often reveal what kind of shoe a person was wearing. Prints can show how the person walks. **Forensic scientists** may guess a suspect's height and weight from a print. Tire tracks can show a vehicle's size, weight, **brand**, and design. All of these details help narrow down the list of suspects in a case.

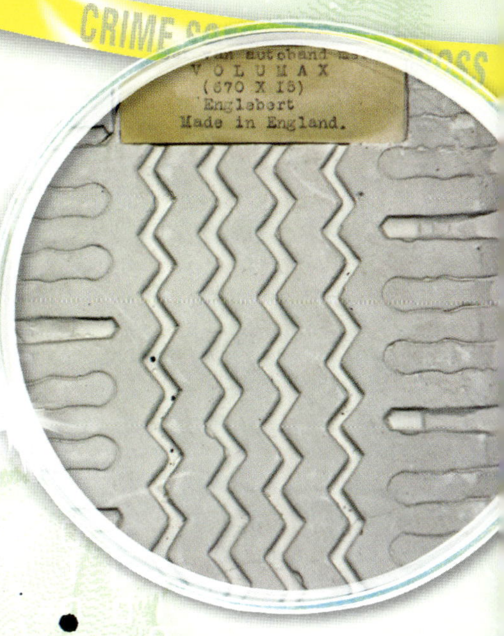

CASE FILE

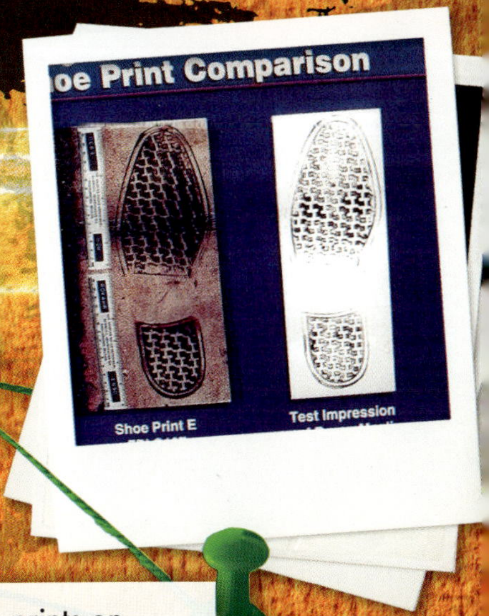

CRIME murder of Nicole Brown Simpson and Ronald Goldman

YEAR OF THE CRIME 1994

HOW IT WAS SOLVED Investigators found bloody shoe prints on the sidewalk near Simpson's home. The shoe prints were from a size 12 Bruno Magli brand shoe. A photo was discovered of the suspect at a football game wearing the same style of shoes that left the prints. This evidence was important in the civil trial that found the suspect responsible for the murders.

CSIs take photos of the crime scene from many angles. They take wide photos of the entire scene to show where patterns are located. Other photos are taken directly over the pattern. CSIs also take close-up photos. These photos show pattern details and measurements such as a suspect's shoe size.

STEADY PHOTOS

CSIs use tripods for some pattern photos. Tripods help get an exact angle on a print. They keep the camera steady for clear photos.

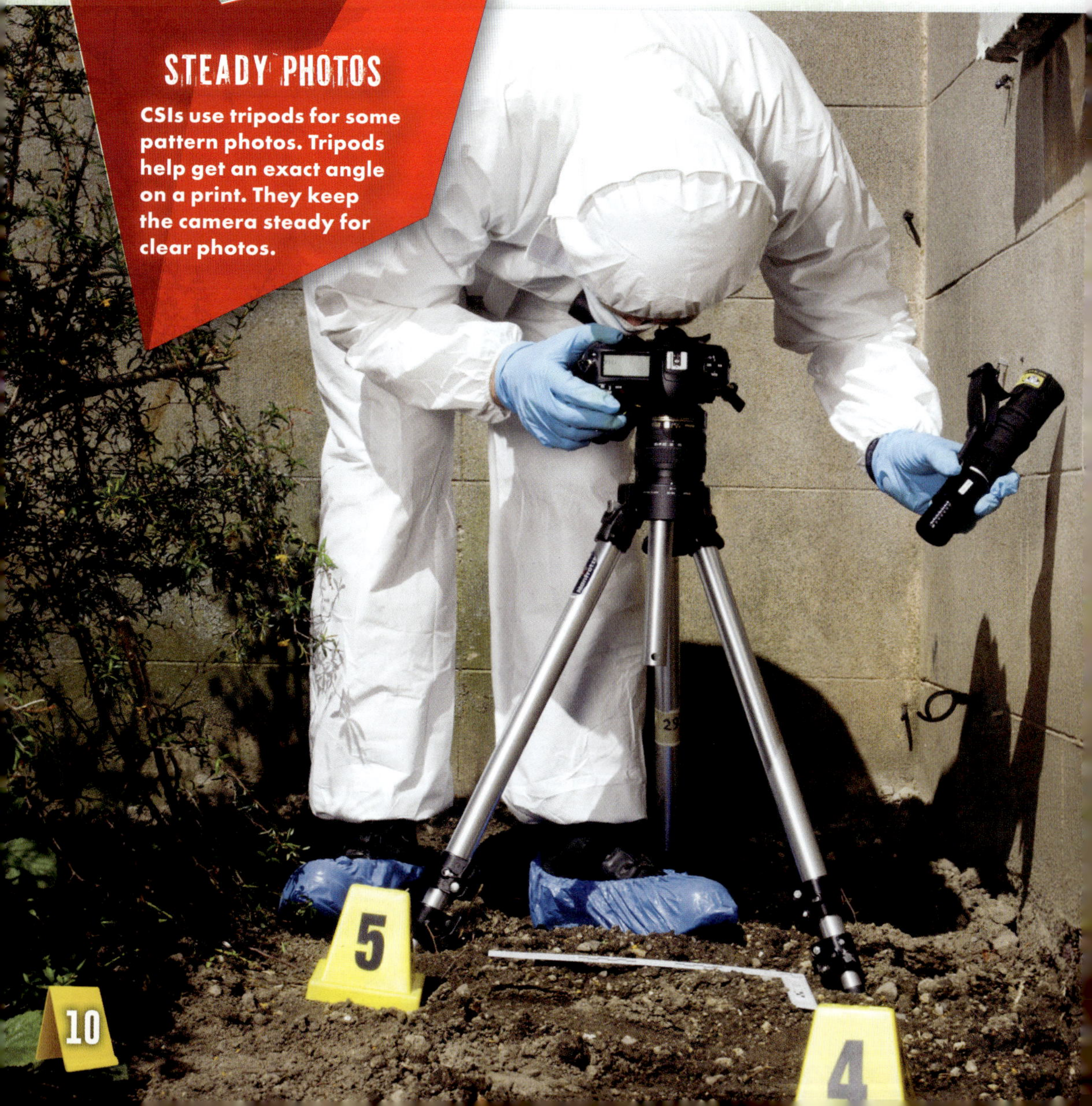

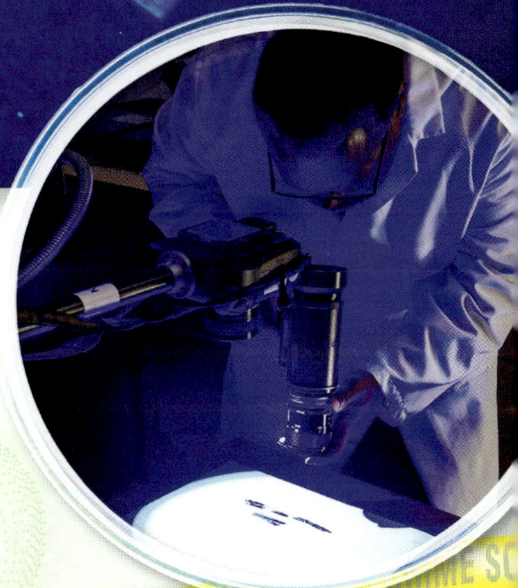

CSIs often use chemicals or lights while taking photos. These help them capture more details. CSIs find latent patterns by shining a light diagonally at the ground. Ridges in footprints and tire tracks cast tiny shadows that make prints visible.

CSIs may capture holograms of latent footprints. Holograms are like photographs that create 3D images. Lasers are used to record the print. This method works for footprints on carpets.

AT THE DENTIST!

CSIs often use dental stone for casting footprints or tire tracks. This is what dentists use to make molds for braces and dentures.

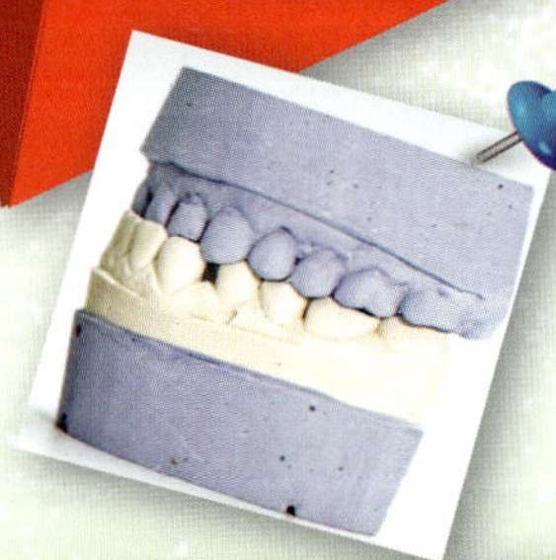

Casting is used to pick up plastic prints. These prints are often pressed into soft or wet surfaces. CSIs start by mixing powdered stone with water. They pour the mix into the pattern. They let it dry and harden. Then they carefully remove the cast from the pattern. The result is a 3D **model**!

FOOTPRINT 3D MODEL

PREPARING SNOW FOR FOOTPRINT CASTING

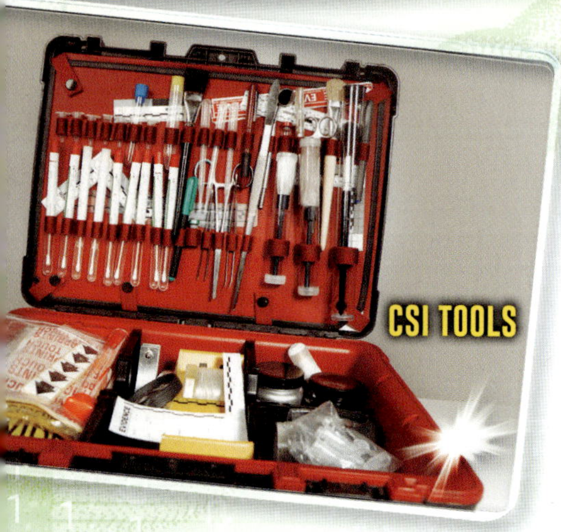

CSIs have many tools for collecting pattern evidence. They use special thin tape. The tape picks up patterns from tile or wood floors. It also works on metal counters. **Gelatin lifters** are also helpful tools. They bend easily. CSIs use them to lift patterns from smooth, rough, and curved surfaces.

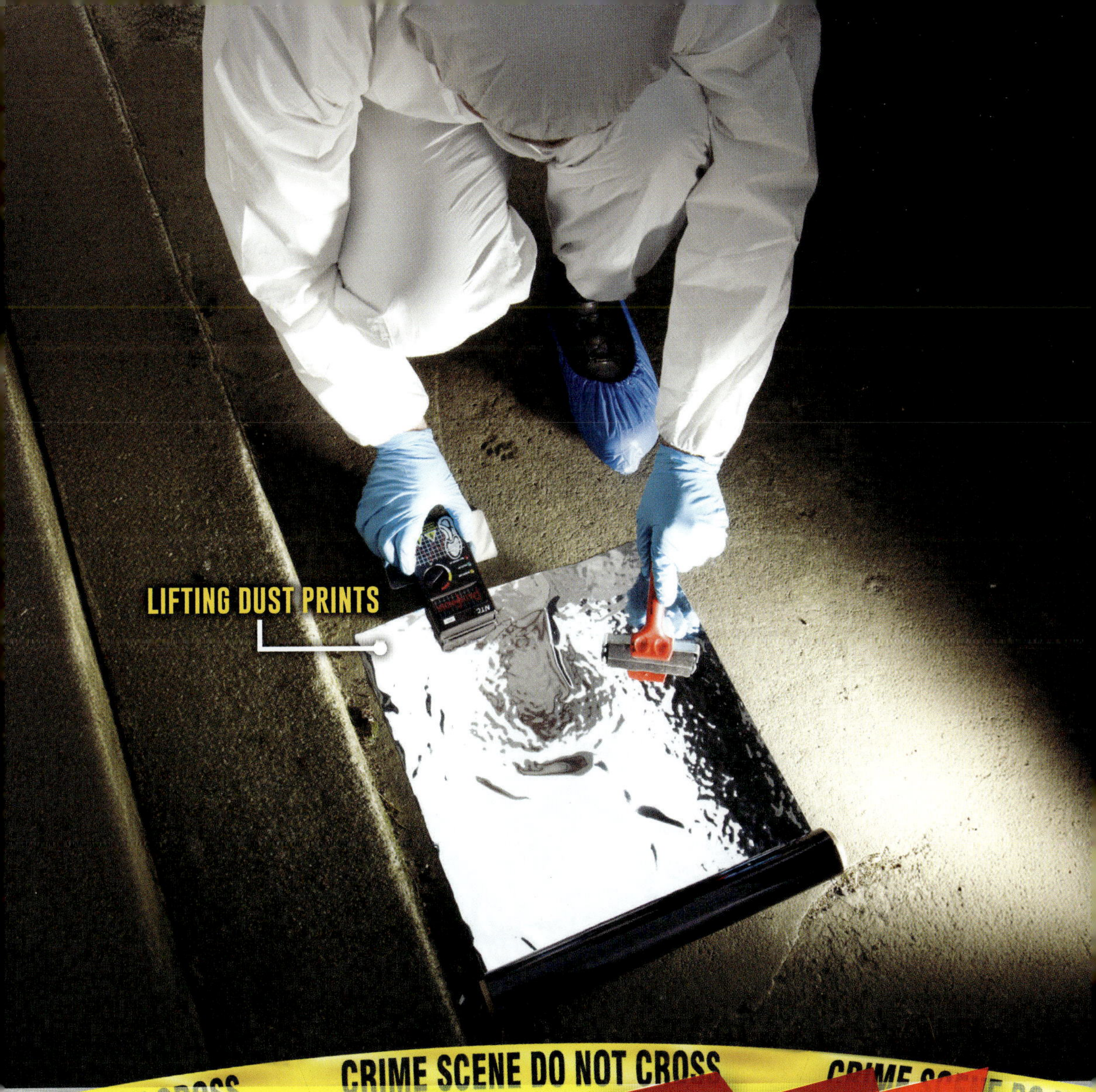

Dust-print lifting tools use static electricity. They attract small pieces of dust. The pieces stay on the tool's sticky surface. This method captures prints made by dry, clean shoes.

TOE PRINTS!

Bare feet leave latent prints. Their patterns can be analyzed just like fingerprints!

There are many challenges and moving parts to a crime scene. This can lead to evidence damage. Police and others working at the scene can accidentally wipe out patterns. Weather can also quickly erase footprints and tire tracks. Even undamaged tire tracks can be hard to match to specific vehicles.

It takes hard work to find, collect, and **analyze** pattern evidence. But it is worth it! CSIs use pattern evidence to understand what happened and who was at the crime scene.

CHALLENGES

WEATHER DAMAGE AT OUTDOOR CRIME SCENES

ACCIDENTAL DAMAGE

POOR QUALITY PRINTS

SOLVING THE CRIME

FLOORING TO THE LAB!

Sometimes CSIs remove a piece of flooring with important footprint evidence. Forensic labs study these original visible prints.

CSIs send collected footprints and tire patterns to a **forensic laboratory**, or lab. Forensic scientists use tools to analyze patterns. They work with **microscopes**. They use special lights. They also use calipers. These tools help scientists get exact measurements.

Scientists analyze patterns in two ways. They look for class features. These include brands, sizes, and general tread patterns. Then they look for individual features. These are unique marks on shoes or tires. These marks help connect patterns to suspects.

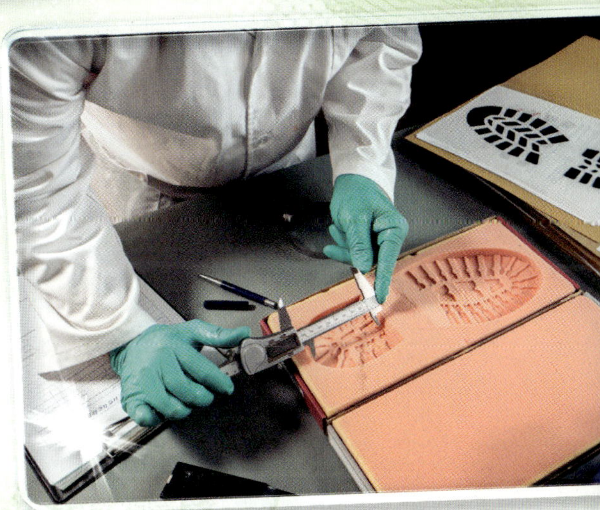

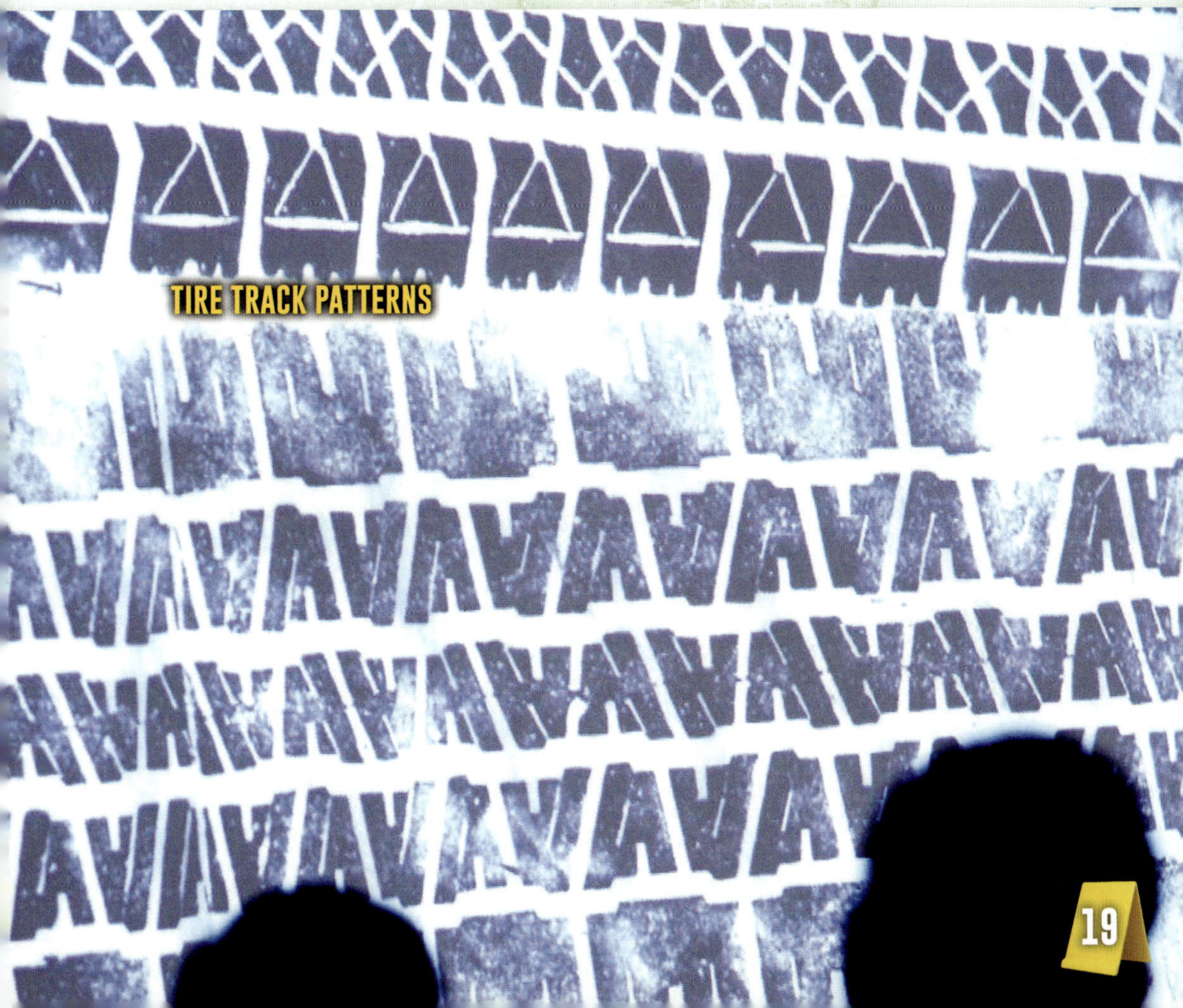

TIRE TRACK PATTERNS

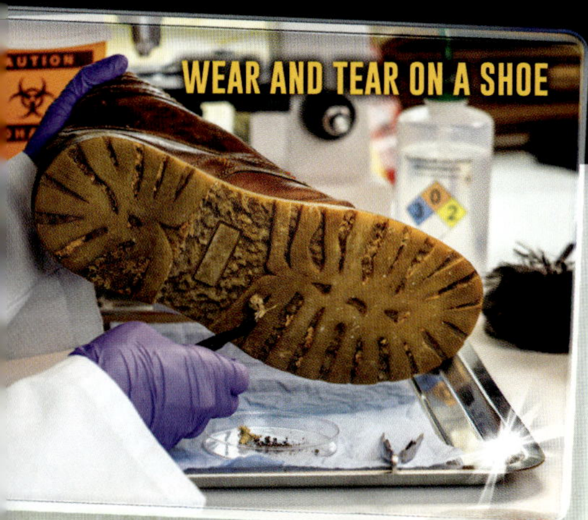

WEAR AND TEAR ON A SHOE

Scientists look for unique signs of wear and tear. They use **software** to see tiny details in crime scene photos. Some details might be nicks or cuts. Other details can be areas that are more worn.

Databases help scientists compare evidence to previous shoe and tire records. Scientists upload their pattern images to databases. They search lists of shoes and tire tracks that have created similar patterns. Database results include helpful resources such as photos, videos, and shoe or tire design information. Scientists use these details to guide their pattern analysis.

Scientists decide if patterns connect to a suspect. They might decide the patterns do not belong to a suspect. They might decide the evidence has a "strong association." This means a suspect could have made the print. Scientists may say the suspect's shoe or tire positively did make the print.

Sometimes the evidence is poor quality or inconclusive. Scientists cannot know if a pattern belongs to a suspect.

Another scientist reviews each piece of pattern evidence. They confirm the results. Scientists write a report about the patterns. They share their conclusions with CSIs.

Pattern evidence is often used in criminal cases. It helps police piece together details about the crime. Muddy shoe prints can reveal how many suspects were at the scene. Tire tracks might show how the suspects left the scene.

If a criminal case goes to trial, forensic scientists may serve as expert witnesses. Lawyers present the evidence. Scientists explain their pattern results. Lawyers ask the scientists questions. A judge or jury decides if there is enough evidence to **convict** a suspect.

LAWYER WITH EVIDENCE

CASE FILE

TIRE TRACK EVIDENCE

CRIME burglary

YEAR OF THE CRIME 2021

HOW IT WAS SOLVED A burglar stole over $5,000 worth of items from a home. He left muddy footprints and muddy tire tracks at the crime scene. Police followed the tire tracks to a nearby house. They found the muddy boots on the porch and a truck in the driveway. The boot prints matched the muddy prints at the scene. Police searched the home and found the stolen items!

THE FUTURE OF FOOTPRINT AND TIRE TRACK FORENSICS

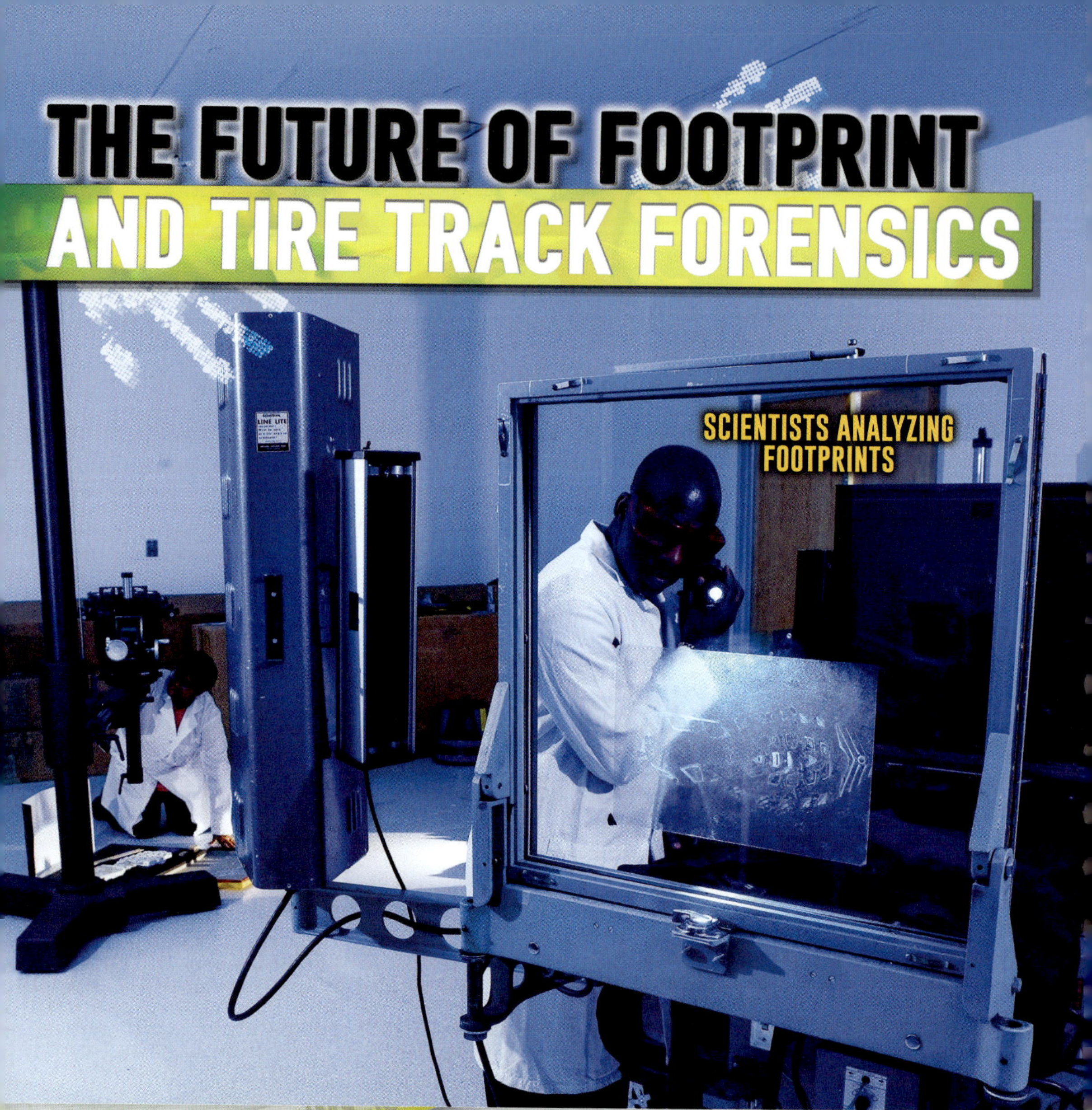

SCIENTISTS ANALYZING FOOTPRINTS

Technology advances have improved pattern evidence analysis in recent years. CSIs need clear pattern images. Casting at the scene takes time. They use a technology called digital fringe projection. It takes 3D images that catch even more detail than casting. The tool is easy to move. Any CSI can use it!

CSIs also have tools that analyze the chemical "fingerprint" of tire rubber. These tools help CSIs make a chemical record of tire marks. This record can help link a car or truck to a crime scene.

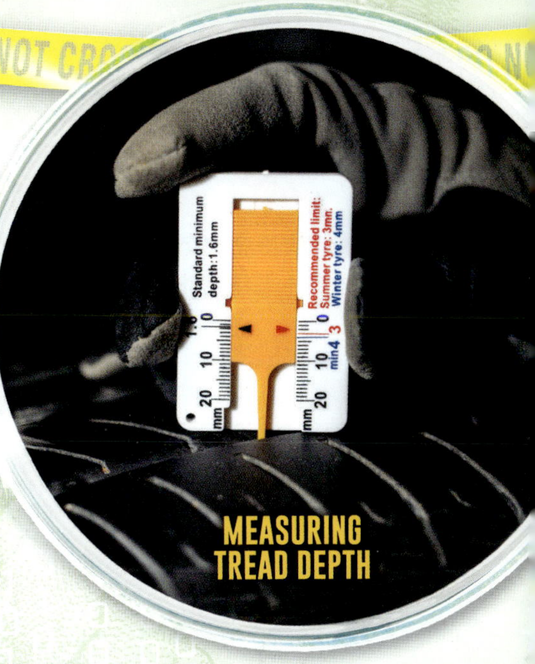

MEASURING TREAD DEPTH

DRONES

YEAR INVENTED

first used by police around

2005

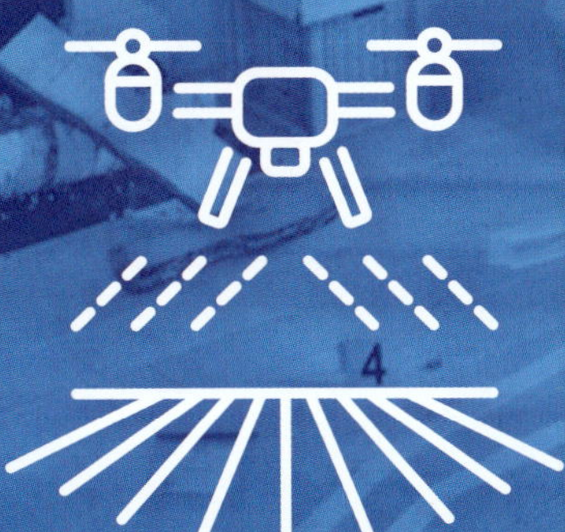

HOW THEY WORK

Drones can carry cameras and lasers. They take 3D images of crime scenes. They gather high-quality images of footprints, tire tracks, and other evidence. Drones rarely damage evidence.

Artificial intelligence (AI) is now used to study pattern evidence. AI tools can scan and match patterns. These tools work well when patterns are partial or hard to read. They are highly accurate in correctly identifying matching prints. They can work much faster than a human studying footprints or tire tracks.

SHOE PRINT COMPARISON USING AI

ADDING A LIFTED FOOTPRINT PATTERN TO AN AI DATABASE

Scientists are careful as they use AI in forensic labs. AI can be **biased**. It depends on the data given to the AI tool. Scientists are working to make the tools more fair. AI can be a powerful tool for scientists. It helps them solve cases faster. Case closed!

GLOSSARY

2D—two-dimensional; showing length and width.

3D—three-dimensional; showing length, width, height, and depth.

analyze—to look carefully at something to understand and identify its important parts

artificial intelligence—a computer's ability to do things a human mind can do

biased—giving results that favor certain characteristics or outcomes

brand—a category of products all made by the same company

casting—the process of pouring a substance into a space to create a 3D model of the shape

convict—to find someone guilty of a crime

crime scene investigators—people who collect and analyze evidence found at crime scenes

databases—digital systems used to store and sort data

evidence—a witness statement or an item or impression found at a crime scene that links a suspect to a crime

forensic laboratory—a place where scientists perform tests to study evidence left at a crime scene

forensic scientists—people who use scientific methods to study physical evidence

gelatin lifters—sheets made of gelatin and rubber that are used to pick up pattern evidence

microscopes—laboratory tools that make tiny things look much bigger

model—an exact copy of an object or pattern

software—computer programs that do specific tasks

suspect—a person the police believe may have committed a crime

TO LEARN MORE

AT THE LIBRARY

Cooper, Chris. *Eyewitness Forensic Science*. New York, N.Y.: DK Publishing, 2020.

Messner, Kate, and Anne Ruppert. *Solve This! Forensics*. Washington, D.C.: National Geographic, 2020.

Ross, Melissa B. *Forensics for Kids: The Science and History of Crime Solving with 21 Activities*. Chicago, Ill.: Chicago Review Press, 2022.

ON THE WEB

FACTSURFER

Factsurfer.com gives you a safe, fun way to find more information.

1. Go to www.factsurfer.com.
2. Enter "footprints and tire tracks" into the search box and click .
3. Select your book cover to see a list of related content.

INDEX

The images in this book are reproduced through the courtesy of: Couperfield, front cover, pp. 4-5, 8, 11 (top), 14 (top), 25; Jeff McCollough, pp. 2 (evidence marker 1), 3 (evidence marker 3); Uri, p. 3 (evidence marker 2); Arthur Tanner/ Fox Photos/ Getty Images, p. 5; Alisusha, pp. 6, 17; jacoblund, p. 6 (bottom); Jim Varney/ Science Source Images, pp. 7, 10, 14, 15 (top); US Geological Service/ Wikimedia Commons, p. 7 (stats top); New Africa, p. 7 (stats middle); Gorodenkoff, p. 7 (stats bottom); D-Keine, p. 8 (bottom); Clement Philippe/ Alamy Stock Photo, p. 9 (top); SUSAN STERNER/ AP Images, p. 9; FBI media/ Federal Bureau of Investigation, pp. 11, 12, 13, 18, 26, 27; Zakharchuk, p. 12 (bottom); FotoDax, p. 13 (top); krstrbrt, p. 15; Max Acronym, p. 16 (top); Prath, pp. 16, 17 (top right); Mickys, p. 17 (top left); Maryna Marchenko, p. 17 (bottom); Don Himsel/ AP Images, p. 19; BSIP/ Universal Images Group/ Getty Images, pp. 20-21; DIGICOMPHOTO, pp. 19 (top), 20, 22, 23; Dominick Reuter/ AP Images, p. 24; Robert King/ Newsmakers/ Getty Images, p. 25 (top); ronstik, p. 27 (top); guteksk7, p. 28 (computer); Andreas Arnold/ picture alliance/ Getty Images, p. 28 (screen); Andreas Arnold/ Getty Images, p. 29.